Contents

Introduction to Dynamics

The musical element of DYNAMICS is about recognising and creating loud and quiet sounds (or phrases), and silences in a piece of music. These sounds (or phrases) can be reproduced using bodies, voices, and instruments. A piece of music or a song can be performed loudly or quietly or at any volume in between—or with varying dynamics for special effects. (See *Tell me where*, p.10.) Some of the most interesting compositions will have a great deal of dynamic contrast.

Musical sounds

This book on the musical element of DYNAMICS explores the use of instruments (including the voice) which can be used to make loud and quiet sounds. Most instruments can produce both, depending on how they are played, although it can be difficult to produce sounds that get gradually louder or quieter, for example, with a maraca (shaker). (See *I'm loud, you're quiet*, p.7, and *Tell me what*, p.13.) Allow the children to experiment and use their imaginations when playing instruments. Hands and bodies will also make loud and quiet sounds.
(*See Don't keep it to yourself*, p.8.)
Don't forget to think about silences: they can be enormously effective in all manner of situations . . .
The Golden Rule is helpful—anything goes as long as it doesn't hurt the player, their friends or the instrument!
Accidents can happen however, and everything wears out in time even though there may be little money to replace them. Poor quality (and home-made) instruments don't last long, so buy the best you can afford—one good tambourine is a much better investment than six cheap and tinny ones which make cheap and tinny little noises.

Putting it into practice

A major aim of this book is to encourage the pupils to think for themselves—
- when choosing appropriate instruments and sounds
- when starting and stopping
- generally when taking control of their music

For this reason there is an emphasis on applauding: not because everything produced is excellent, but because the performer is sharing something of themselves with the audience, which listens silently and then thanks them with a round of applause. At this point you can ask players and listeners—
- which part of the music they liked the best—and why
- how well the instructions were carried out
- whether there were any parts that could be improved next time round

Valuing the children's efforts is an important part of helping them to learn.

Equally vital is that there are opportunities to experiment alone with sounds. In today's classroom this can be difficult, but a music corner with games the children have already experienced doesn't have to be 'open' all the time (especially with drums on a wet Friday . . .), and older pupils are frequently capable of working outside the room. Do, however, listen to their efforts with the whole class. The use of an adult helper to keep an eye on things can forestall trouble, but ensure their role as a supervisor is understood and ask them not to join in with their own musical suggestions.

One of the few times to get involved however, is when 'perpetual motion' has set in during a performance, and the player has started, but can't stop. Don't allow the child to flounder, but break in with loud clapping. Next time give the instruction 'and when your music is finished, put the instrument down'. Making musical choices can often turn the brain to cotton wool too, but you can get everyone out of a difficult situation by asking if a friend can help the child.

These games and activities are for having fun, but not for uncontrolled chaos. If things get noisy, don't grab the biggest cymbal and give it a whack—the class will only respond by getting even noisier—give a quiet clap and raise your hand instead. You might have to wait until everyone notices, but it never fails in the end.

Echo my leader

Listening skills
Recognising louds and quiets in sounds made
by voices

- Explain to the class that you are going to whisper several words, asking them to echo each word after you.

- Instead of whispering the final word, say it very loudly.

- Ask everyone to sit up again and talk about how you used your voice quietly and loudly.

Developments

▶ Play this game around a circle: everyone whispers a word except the previously chosen volunteer who shouts one. *If this person is chosen by touch when everyone has their eyes shut it adds a surprise element.*

▶ Practise the days of the week, months, or spelling out words: echo the leader who whispers the letters and says just one letter of the word very loudly.

Link with
I'm loud,
you're quiet, p.7

room to sit comfortably in a circle

I'm loud, you're quiet

Making loud and quiet sounds with voices
Creating repeating patterns

■ Sitting in a circle if possible, ask the children to whisper their own name in turn.

■ Now try this again, asking alternate children to say their name loudly. Look at the repeating pattern by asking all the louds to stand up.

■ Make other repeating patterns such as quiet, quiet, loud, and look at the result.

Developments

▶ All say 'hello' or use topic-related words.

▶ Ask a pupil to suggest the loud/quiet pattern to be made.

▶ Count around the circle in 2s, or practise other times tables, *e.g. 3 times table: every '3' has to be said very loudly.*

Link with
Echo my leader, p.6

You will need

room to sit
comfortably
in a circle

Don't keep it to yourself

Listening skills
Passing loud and quiet hand sounds around a circle

- Sitting in a circle, pass a single clap around.
  Can everyone wait for their turn?

Developments

▶ Ask a pupil to start the game.

▶ Pass it in the opposite direction.

▶ Look at the person you pass it to.

▶ Can it be done with eyes shut?

▶ Pass a quiet clap. Pass a loud clap followed by a quiet one—and talk about what happened. (The two always end up the same the first time you play the game!)

▶ Invent other sounds to pass around, some loud, some quiet.

▶ Pass three sounds, *e.g. clap, click, knee tap.*

▶ Try passing two different sounds—both in the same direction, and then in opposite ones. *Start with a clap, and when six or seven pupils have passed it on, start a knee tap going.* Talk about why this is difficult.

Link with
Tell me what, p.13,
Conduct a friend, p.16

room to sit
comfortably

enough room
for one person to
move around safely

Follow me

Listening skills
Loud and quiet sounds around us

*You will need to stress that absolute silence is needed
for this game to work properly.*

- With their eyes shut, ask the class to point to
  your footsteps, as you walk around the room.
  Talk to them in the first instance so that
  everyone is pointing in the right direction
  when they open their eyes. *There's too much
  failure and fear of getting it wrong, and it's nice
  to know once in a while you are guaranteed
  to be right!*

- Talk about sounds being quieter when
  far away.

Developments

▶ Choose a volunteer with noisy feet to be the
leader with you.

▶ Walk silently to another spot and then clap
once. Who can point to where you are now?
Instead of clapping, make a quieter sound.
Can everyone still tell where you are?
Why is this harder?

Link with
Tell me where, p.10

Tell me where

You will need

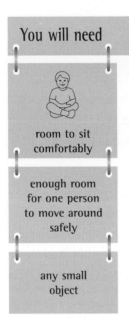

room to sit comfortably

enough room for one person to move around safely

any small object

Listening skills
Creating loud and quiet sounds collaboratively with hands

A good game to use just before playtime.

- Choose a volunteer to be the 'searcher'. He/she should be out of sight while you hide a small object in the room.

- Allow the searcher to come back into the room. Ask everyone to help the searcher find it by clapping gradually louder and louder as s/he moves towards it, and quieter as they move away.

Young children will need the assistance of an adult to move in different directions.

Developments

▶ Ask a child to hide the object.

▶ Use other body sounds.

Link with
Follow me, p.9

room to sit
comfortably in
a circle

tambourine
(and small selection
of other
instruments)

Silence is golden

Trying to create silences with instruments

- Sitting in a circle, try to pass a tambourine around absolutely silently. It's impossible. Discuss why. *The jingles aren't fixed so they always rattle.*

- Find other 'impossible' instruments.

Developments

▶ When putting instruments away at the end of the activity, try asking the children to do it one at a time quite silently. It has a noticeably calming effect, and you can talk about why some instruments are easy and others not. *After playing this game there is never any excuse for anyone to play an instrument when they have been asked not to!*

Link with
Silent hands and sheep, p.19,
Stressed sheep, p.23

Cat and mouse

Listening skills
Using an instrument to create loud and quiet
sounds

■ The cat plays a tambourine very quietly as your
class of mice peep from behind their whiskers.
Beware! It's going to pounce!! Everyone must
hide their faces when the tambourine is tapped
loudly.

Developments

▶ Ask a child to be the cat.

▶ Use another instrument which can play both
loudly and quietly easily—does its sound
suggest any other animal?

Link with
Feely bag
and beads, pp.14–15,
Little and large, p.17

You will need

room to sit
comfortably

a choice of 3
percussion
instruments

Tell me what

Working collaboratively
Creating loud and quiet sounds on instruments

Loud playing can get very over-enthusiastic. The Golden Rule is helpful:

> You can do anything you like with any of the instruments as long as it doesn't hurt you, your friend, or the instrument.

This covers every conceivable possibility!

■ Pick two friends or confident children. One should tell the other whether to play loudly or quietly using one from the choice of three instruments in the centre.

■ Let the player have a short 'fiddle' and then ask them to play 'beautiful music' in this way and to put the instrument down when the music is finished so the class can applaud.

■ Some instruments are easier than others to play loudly, some easier to play quietly. Discuss why this is so.

Developments

▶ Invent new ways of playing instruments quietly (or loudly).

▶ Choose a leader who should invent signs that mean 'loud' and 'quiet'. Ask the players to follow the different signs.

▶ Ask for music that gradually gets louder/quieter. This is hard and will need practice. You can help the player by conducting, *e.g. move hands together and apart.*

Link with
Don't keep it
to yourself, p.8,
Conduct a friend, p.16

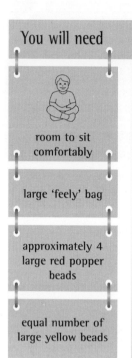

room to sit
comfortably

large 'feely' bag

approximately 4
large red popper
beads

equal number of
large yellow beads

Feely bag and beads

Using voices to create loud and quiet sounds
Reading from a graphic score

*My 'feely' bag is shaped like a large tiger. On a bad
day it growls as a hand is put in its mouth. . .*

■ In a large bag put several big 'popper' beads
of the two different colours (as used with early
years). Ask individuals to feel the bag and
discuss what might be inside. *Multi-link is a
good alternative.*

■ Without looking, pull out one bead. Tell the
children that this colour means 'make a loud
sound'. Everyone should say the word 'loud'
very loudly when you point at the bead.

■ Remove another bead: if the same colour, the
children say 'loud' again. If the second colour,
they should be asked to say 'quiet' in a whisper
as you point at it.

■ Remove a third bead (or until the second
colour appears), and then pop them together
to make a short piece of music. Read this
graphic score (or notation).

■ Continue until all the beads are used up,
perhaps asking for brave volunteers to take out
the beads.

Developments

▶ What happens if the 'necklace' is turned over? Will the music sound the same?

▶ Arrange the beads in a repeating pattern.

▶ Ask for a volunteer to compose another necklace by re-arranging the beads.

▶ Choose someone to play the 'necklace' using an instrument—allow the opportunity to play a loud and a quiet sound before attempting the music.

▶ Add a third colour for 'make a silence'.

▶ A good game for pairs using four colours and 2 instruments in the music corner.

Link with
Cat and mouse, p.12,
Little and large, p.17

Conduct a friend

Working collaboratively
Creating quiet sounds and silences using
instruments

Use several instruments on which the players have
had the opportunity to discover loud and quiet
sounds.

- Discuss with the children how a conductor
  gives directions to an orchestra or choir
  without any vocal instructions.

- Pick one player per instrument and then the
  conductor who invents a sign that means 'play
  quietly' and another meaning 'stop'. Who will
  the conductor signal to play first? Can
  everyone wait their turn?

- Ask the conductor to invent a sign that means
  'play loudly'.

Developments

▶ Find signs that mean 'gradually play louder'
  and 'gradually quieter and quieter'.

▶ Ask the conductor to find a way of adding
  players one by one (no voice directions
  allowed) and talk about how the music gets
  louder as more players are added.

▶ Can s/he discover a way to make the music get
  quieter?

▶ Play the game with *groups* of instrumentalists
  not just soloists.

▶ A good game for the music corner.

Link with
Don't keep it
to yourself, p.8,
Tell me what, p.13

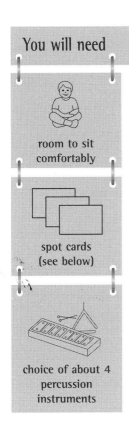

You will need

room to sit
comfortably

spot cards
(see below)

choice of about 4
percussion
instruments

Link with

Cat and mouse, p.12,
Feely bag and beads,
pp.14–15

Little and large

*Using hands, bodies and instruments to create loud
and quiet sounds*
Reading from a graphic score

■ Copy the spot cards (or photocopy and enlarge
those given below) onto individual pieces of
card. A large spot means 'make a loud sound',
and a small spot, a quiet one.

■ Play the spot cards one by one with the class.
Decide whether to use hand, body, or
instrumental sounds. Remember to pick
instruments that can play both loudly and
quietly easily. *Allow a little 'fiddling' time
beforehand to ensure the solo player can control
the instrument well enough to play in both ways.*

Developments

▶ Different coloured spots could mean other
instruments.

▶ Arrange the cards in a row for a longer piece of
music—a graphic score or notation.

▶ A good game for the music corner.

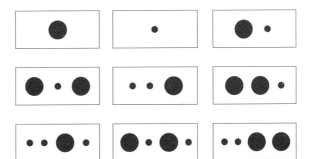

Stop-go

Things to do with almost any very well-known song

Using voices to make sounds and silences in a song

■ Together with the class, sing 'Baa baa black sheep' or any very well-known song using a stop-go card. *One side should be green meaning 'sing'; the other should be red meaning 'think the words'.*

■ Start with the green 'sing' side showing. When you flip the sign to red, the children should internalise the words until you flip to green again. *Everyone should start singing again on the correct word. If you mouth the words obviously in the silent parts then everyone will get it right.*

Developments

▶ Use a child as the leader.

▶ Invent hand signs that mean 'sing' and 'internalise'—for example, a raised or lowered thumb. Ask the children for their ideas.

▶ Use the same game with any very well-known song.

▶ Use the stop-go card for other occasions, for example, to conduct or for applause.

Link with
Silence is golden, p.11,
Silent hands
and a sheep, p.19

room to sit
comfortably

any well-known
song the class
enjoys singing

Silent hands
and a sheep

Things to do with almost any very well-known song

Silent movements to the beat and pulse of a song

- Together with the class sing 'Baa baa black sheep' or any other very well-known song while tapping knees silently to the beat. *This beat or pulse continues throughout (or should do) without wavering or getting tangled up with the words: just like our own heartbeats which keep going at more or less the same speed whatever we're doing.*

- Ask for suggestions for other silent movements.

- Count how many beats there are in each line. *This gives the metre of the music. Most songs have two or four, some such as 'Oranges and lemons' have three.*

- Invent an easy pattern of repeated silent movements to match the number of beats and make these as the song is sung again.

Developments

▶ Do something different to each line of the song.

▶ Try a verse with movements only and the words internalised.

▶ Invent repeated patterns of silent movements and quiet body sounds. Ask the pupils for their ideas.

Link with
Silence is golden, p.11,
Stressed sheep, p.23

A little bit of Italian

Learning about some common musical terms for dynamics
Creating loud and quiet music using body sounds

■ Copy these Italian words onto individual cards, or photocopy and enlarge the cards given opposite. On the reverse write the abbreviation and the English meaning.

| forte | f loud | piano | p quiet |

■ Introduce the cards to the class and ask for a body sound to be made for as long as the card is raised (incorporating the dynamic given).

Developments

▶ Use other body/hand sounds or an instrument.

▶ Write the words in different colours for different sounds or instruments.

▶ Arrange a line of the cards and play the music as the conductor points at each card.

▶ Use one card per line to sing a very well-known song.

▶ Ask a child to be the composer and arrange the cards—and to be the conductor too.

▶ Perform the finished music to another class.

▶ A good game for the music corner.

▶ Introduce these additional words when everyone is confident with the first two:

fortissimo, pianissimo, crescendo, diminuendo, niente.

forte	f loud
piano	p quiet
fortissimo	ff very loud
pianissimo	pp very quiet
crescendo	$cresc <$ gradually getting louder
diminuendo	$dim >$ gradually getting quieter
niente	dying away to silence

Accents

Making accents using hands and voices within a repeating steady beat

- With the class, count steadily from one to four repeatedly, saying the number '1' loudly each time. Add a loud clap on '1' and quiet claps on the other numbers. *This is the metre; i.e. when the steady beat or pulse can be felt in repeating groups. The first in each group always feels stronger. By clapping loudly on '1' we are accenting this number.*

- Do the same with, for example, groups of 2, 3, 5, and 6 beats.

Developments

- Use other body sounds—ask for the pupils' ideas.

- Add an instrument on number '1' to make the accent even more noticeable.

- Write a line of numbers and perform each number group once—without stopping! *e.g. count 1, 2; 1, 2, 3; 1, 2 . . . Remember to clap each time you say '1'.*

- Try in two groups, each with different numbers.

- While singing a very well-known song try to perform one of these accented number groups—5 is always difficult!

Link with
Silent hands and
a sheep, p.19,
Stressed sheep, p.23

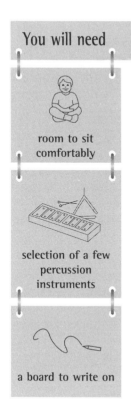
Stressed sheep

Things to do with almost any very well-known song

Making accents using hands and instruments

- With the class, whisper 'Baa baa black sheep' or any very well-known song, gently clapping along with the rhythm of the words. When this is secure ask everyone to internalise the words so that only the quiet clapping can be heard.

- Help the children choose one word per line which is to be stressed—accented—and write these words on the board for everyone to see. *The children may find it easier to see the words of the whole song, with the accented words underlined.*

- Quietly clap the words of the song, accenting the chosen words by clapping these loudly. *Young children will probably simply <u>have</u> to shout these words as well as clap them loudly!*

- Choose one or more volunteers to play the accented words on instruments and add these to the game.

Developments

▶ Perform the game to another class, or make a tape. Can they work out which words have accents just by listening?

▶ Choose two words per line to accent.

▶ Play the same game with any very well-known song.

Link with
Accents, p.22

You will need

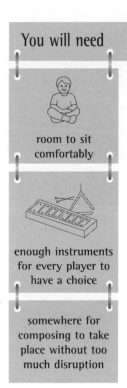

room to sit
comfortably

enough instruments
for every player to
have a choice

somewhere for
composing to take
place without too
much disruption

Link with
Tell me what, p.13,
Little and large, p.17,
A little bit of Italian,
pp.20–21

From here to there and back again

A composing activity for small groups

- With the class talk about how music can be made louder by playing a single instrument more loudly or by increasing the number of performers, and made quieter by playing an instrument more quietly or reducing the number of performers.

- Divide the class into small groups of about five players and tell each group they are to compose a piece of music in three sections:
  The beginning should change from the quietest possible sounds to loud, or from loud to quiet — *remember not to hurt yourselves or the instruments*; the middle should contain a surprise for the audience; the ending should be as different as possible from the beginning.

- Allow enough time for each group to rehearse and polish their music, and then perform the finished pieces to the rest of the class.

- Talk about the pieces with the children—did everyone follow the instructions? Were there any brilliant or surprising ideas?

Developments

▶ Give the music a title—before or after the composing is finished.

▶ Ask the groups to include other contrasts such as fast/slow or long/short sounds.

▶ A suitable activity for small groups working towards a 'grand sharing' at the end of the week.